GENIUS
SCIENTISTS
AND THEIR
GENIUS IDEAS

COPERNICUS

GENIUS OF MODERN ASTRONOMY

Catherine M. Andronik

Enslow Publishers, Inc.
40 Industrial Road
Box 398
Berkeley Heights, NJ 07922
USA

http://www.enslow.com

For Holy Cross School in New Britain, Connecticut
—and for Mom

Originally published as *Copernicus: Founder of Modern Astronomy* in 2009.

Library of Congress Cataloging-in-Publication Data

Andronik, Catherine M., author.
  Copernicus : genius of modern astronomy / Catherine M. Andronik.
    pages cm. — (Genius scientists and their genius ideas)
  "Originally published as Copernicus : founder of modern astronomy, revised edition, in 2009."
  Audience: Grades 4-6.
  Includes bibliographical references and index.
  ISBN 978-0-7660-6550-5 — ISBN 0-7660-6550-2 1. Copernicus, Nicolaus, 1473-1543—
Juvenile literature. 2. Astronomers—Poland—Biography—Juvenile literature. 3. Astronomy—
History—Juvenile literature. I. Title.
  QB36.C8A68 2015
  520.92—dc23
                                    2014031249

Future Editions:
Paperback ISBN 978-0-7660-6551-2
EPUB ISBN 978-0-7660-6552-9
Single-User PDF ISBN 978-0-7660-6553-6
Multi-User PDF ISBN 978-0-7660-6554-3

Printed in the United States of America
102014 Bang Printing, Brainerd, Minn.
10 9 8 7 6 5 4 3 2 1

To Our Readers: We have done our best to make sure all Internet Addresses in this book were active and appropriate when we went to press. However, the author and the publisher have no control over and assume no liability for the material available on those Internet sites or on other Web sites they may link to. Any comments or suggestions can be sent by e-mail to comments@enslow.com or to the address on the back cover.

♻Enslow Publishers, Inc., is committed to printing our books on recycled paper. The paper in every book contains 10% to 30% post-consumer waste (PCW). The cover board on the outside of each book contains 100% PCW. Our goal is to do our part to help young people and the environment too!

Illustration Credits: ©Clipart.com, p. 27; Shutterstock.com, ©Tomasz Bidermann, p. 57; ©Thinkstock/Photos.com, p. 1.

Cover Illustration Credits: Shutterstock.com: ©Marish(lightbulb icon); ©Thinkstock, David Szabo/ iStock (solar system).

CONTENTS

Contents

Chapter 1

AWAKENING IDEAS

It was a cold November day in 1520. Fierce knights rode on horseback across a plain of northern Poland. Ahead lay the town of Olsztyn, hidden behind its medieval walls. Its inhabitants had heard of neighboring towns that had fallen to the knights. Many people in these towns had been driven from their homes or killed. Houses had been burned to the ground. But in Olsztyn, the people would defy the feared Teutonic Knights.

One man was determined to protect the town. He was not a prince. He was not a soldier. He was a scholar and a clergyman named Copernicus. As he followed the approach of the knights, he advised the townspeople to stock up on supplies. He also ordered that the wall surrounding the town be fortified. The Teutonic Knights had a long fight ahead of them if they wanted to conquer Olsztyn.

The Teutonic Knights were founded in the twelfth century. They wore uniforms of white robes marked with a large black cross. Their original purpose had been to care for sick travelers from Germany. Then the Holy Roman Emperor offered the knights land in Central Europe. From the castles they built, the Knights would protect Catholic Europe from attack by barbarian tribes. They would help convert those tribes to Christianity by force. By the fifteenth century, most of Europe was Christian. Barbarians were no longer a threat. Yet the Teutonic Knights were still active. Their goals centered on land and political power. They rode through central Europe, attacking towns.

As the Teutonic Knights closed in, Copernicus sent off a desperate letter to King Sigismund of Poland. He begged for help:

> We ourselves are not sufficiently safeguarded to repel . . . an attack and we fear lest the enemy, who is already so near, should besiege us also. . . . Therefore, we humbly appeal to Your Holy Majesty to . . . come to our aid as quickly as possible and to support us. For we are completely devoted to Your Majesty, even if we were to perish.[1]

The letter fell into the hands of the Teutonic Knights and never reached the king. The Knights went on to attack Olsztyn. They even breached the town gate. But they could not take the town. Thanks to the preparations of Copernicus, Olsztyn was saved.

Life in the time of Copernicus was not all about fighting knights, however. This was also the beginning of the period we call the Renaissance. The name Renaissance comes from the Latin word for "rebirth." During the Renaissance, many Europeans studied Greek and Roman philosophers. They wanted to recapture the spirit of ancient Greece and Rome. The Renaissance represented a rebirth of these cultures. It was an exciting time to be alive. Copernicus was one of many young people who were eager to study and learn.

One of the things that interested the ancient Greek thinkers was the structure of the universe. Many of them spent a great deal of time watching the skies. They observed the heavenly bodies—the moon, the sun, and the stars. The study of the motions of stars and planets is called astronomy. The origins of astronomy can be traced back many thousands of years, but the Greeks were the first ones to catalog all the stars that they could see.

To most ancient thinkers, it seemed logical that they were at the center of the universe. After all, everything appears to revolve around the earth: the sun, the moon, and all the stars. Many different models were proposed to describe the shape of the universe. One model proposed that all the heavenly bodies were set in a series of giant crystal spheres. These spheres all revolved around the earth.

Most accepted this model. But through the ages there were some who challenged it. They suggested that perhaps the earth was not the center of the universe. Perhaps there were no crystal spheres. Perhaps the earth was just another heavenly body, like the planets, suspended in space. Perhaps the earth moved. Some even suggested that the sun might be the center of our universe. Since *helios* is the Greek word for "sun," this theory is called the heliocentric theory. The theory placing the earth at the center is called the geocentric theory. *Geo* is the Greek word for "earth."

Most of the ideas that took the earth out of the center of the universe were never taken seriously. Such ideas defied everything that was plain and obvious. They also implied that the earth and its people did not hold a special place in the universe.

Still, scientists studied the skies. Over time, they began to notice that the motions of certain stars and planets did not make sense. These motions could not be explained by the geocentric theory. Some ignored these strange motions. They called them mysteries of nature. Others added loops and twists to the movements of the spheres to explain them. Still others searched for a new model to fit their observations.

Copernicus was one of those who offered a new model of the universe. He proposed a heliocentric theory of his own. His model departed from the ancient system that prevailed in Western culture for centuries, placing Earth at the center of the universe, and is often regarded as the launching point to modern astronomy. However, this theory did more than just place the sun at the center of the universe. It also proposed that the earth was a planet, and that it revolved around the sun along with the other planets.

Modern astronomy began with this theory. It can even be said that modern science began with it. Without it, Isaac Newton might never have conceived of his law of gravity. Gravity is the force that pulls the planets along their orbits. And without Newton's law of gravity, Einstein might never have conceived his theory of relativity. This theory relates gravity to the shape of the universe. Many of our modern ideas about science begin with the heliocentric model of Copernicus.

Once Copernicus's model was accepted, it changed the way people thought about the world. Suddenly, the earth was not at the center of the universe. In some ways, humankind seemed less important. But in other ways, it was very exciting. The true nature of our universe had begun to reveal itself.

Chapter 2

A Scholarly Youth

Nicolaus Copernicus was born at about four-thirty in the afternoon, on February 19, 1473, to Barbara and Mikolaj Kopernik. Usually we do not know such details about the birth of someone in the fifteenth century. But at some point, an astrologer cast Nicolaus's horoscope. Centuries later, the document was found in a library in Germany.[1] Nicolaus was the youngest of four children. He had two sisters named Barbara and Catherine. His brother, Andrew, was about seven years older than he.[2]

The Kopernik family lived in Torun, Poland. Torun was a town of about 20,000 people.[3] It was an important port on the Vistula River. Ships from all around the world crowded its docks. Mikolaj Kopernik depended on these trading ships. He was a copper merchant. Some believe that the name Kopernik refers to the copper that made the family wealthy. It could also refer to the town of Kopernik. This town was probably the family's original home.[4]

Mikolaj's wife, Barbara, was a Watzelrode. The Watzelrodes were one of the most important families in Torun. Like many families in the area, they were of German ancestry, not Polish. Because of his wife's connections, Mikolaj Kopernik became involved in local government.

The Kopernik family was relatively wealthy. They owned a small but comfortable house in Torun, at 17 St. Anny Street. Today this street is known as Copernicus Street. The family's home is still standing.[5] The Koperniks moved to a larger home near the market square when Nicolaus was seven. In the summer, they also enjoyed outings to their country villa and vineyard.[6] There are no records, but young Nicolaus and Andrew probably attended a school connected to their parish church.

Students in the fifteenth century learned by memorizing and repeating. Teachers lectured from a wide variety of famous books, including the Bible. Printed books were still a luxury. Educated people wrote in Latin rather than in their native languages. Education did not usually emphasize imagination or learning to think for oneself.

When Nicolaus was ten years old, his father died. Fortunately, his uncle stepped in to help the family. Nicolaus's uncle, Lukasz Watzelrode, was his mother's brother. (Sometimes the name is spelled Watzenrode. It was not unusual for the same name to be spelled several ways in the Middle Ages.) Lukasz Watzelrode was a Roman Catholic bishop, in charge of a region called Warmia, in the north of Poland. The bishop of Warmia lived in a large, comfortable castle in the town of Lidzbark.

Lukasz Watzelrode was not humorous or pleasant. He was powerful and respected. His political connections reached the king himself.[7] An air of majesty surrounded him. When dinner was served in Lidzbark Castle, a cannon would be fired.[8] The bishop would enter the dining hall, accompanied by his barking dogs.[9] He would then sit down to eat. The most important people sat near him. The less important people sat at tables farther away.[10]

Bishop Watzelrode could be influential in helping his nephews, Nicolaus and Andrew, get church jobs. But first they needed a good education. The bishop arranged for the two boys to attend the University of Krakow in Poland. The university was at that time over one hundred years old—one of the oldest in Europe. It still exists today. Now it is known as the Jagiellonian University. It was renamed for a Polish king.[11] Nicolaus's sisters were not offered an education beyond grammar school. Girls at that time did not attend college.[12] Barbara became a nun. Catherine got married and raised a family.

As a student, Nicolaus would have to study arithmetic and geometry. He also studied astrology as a part of his education. Astrology is the study of the supposed effect the positions of stars and planets have on people's lives. He would learn to make observations of the planets. He studied when and where heavenly bodies rose and set on each day of the year.

While Nicolaus was a student at the University of Krakow, one of his professors was Albert Brudzewski. Brudzewski's knowledge of astronomy was renowned. Astronomy is the study of the motions of stars and planets. During Nicolaus's years in Krakow, Brudzewski taught philosophy. But sometimes he gave astronomy lectures as well.

Brudzewski had studied with some of the most respected astronomers of his generation. One of them was Johannes Müller, better known as Regiomontanus. Regiomontanus's book charting the positions of the planets was popular among sailors. But in the

Middle Ages, astronomy and astrology were closely linked. Regiomontanus himself was both an astronomer and an astrologer. He cast horoscopes at the court of Emperor Frederick III. According to peasant rumors, Regiomontanus even had a mechanical iron fly to do his errands. It also seemed that he held unconventional beliefs. A letter he once wrote suggested he believed the earth moved.[13]

The University of Krakow had many useful tools for astronomy. There was a celestial globe showing the positions of the stars. There were also two fine astrolabes, instruments used in navigation. And there was a triquetrum, an instrument made of three lengths of wood hinged together. It was used to measure the altitude of objects in the sky. To us, these are not very useful instruments for observing the heavens, but they were the best available at the time. The telescope had not been invented yet. On October 14, 1494, the university held a special assembly so professors could demonstrate this equipment to their students. Nicolaus was probably among them.[14]

While the teenaged Nicolaus was a student in the city of Krakow, word spread of an amazing voyage. A sea captain named Christopher Columbus, searching for a quick trade route to Asia, had made landfall on a previously unknown island. This island was part of the soon-to-be-named America. While Nicolaus was studying the heavens, new worlds were opening up here on Earth.

After studying in Krakow, Nicolaus and Andrew went to Italy. There, they enrolled in the University of Bologna. There is a legend that the young men crossed the Alps on foot. The Alps are a high range of mountains north of Italy. According to legend, they were attacked by robbers along the way.[15] This may or may not be true. We do know that when they arrived in Bologna, they needed to borrow money from a family friend. As the lender wrote to Bishop Lukasz Watzelrode: "After the way of students . . . [the] nephews have suffered great want of money."[16]

Nicolaus was supposed to study law at Bologna, but he concentrated on learning Greek—and more astronomy. In Bologna, he studied with another respected astronomer, Domenico Maria da Novaro. He may have even boarded in his home.[17]

On March 9, 1497, Nicolaus and his teacher made detailed notes as they watched the moon pass in front of the red star Aldebaran. This is called an occultation. An occultation happens when one heavenly body blocks the view of another. This occultation was Copernicus's first recorded observation of the stars.[18]

It was also the first time he noticed that something in the stars did not seem to make sense.

According to the ancient Greek mathematician Ptolemy, the moon moved closer to the earth at certain points in its orbit. But after observing the occultation of Aldebaran, Nicolaus performed some calculations. Based on these calculations, he found that the distance from the earth to the moon did not change as much as Ptolemy said it did.[19]

The year 1500 was marked by great festivities in Rome. The Catholic Church was celebrating a jubilee in honor of the new century. A jubilee is a five-hundred-year anniversary. Nicolaus was one of the 200,000 people[20] who traveled to the great city for the Easter celebrations.[21] In Rome, he studied church law for a year. He may have also given lectures about mathematics. At some point, Nicolaus began calling himself Copernicus. Many educated people changed their surnames to make them sound Latin. Nicolaus changed Kopernik to Copernicus.

With the help of his uncle, Copernicus was given a job in the Church. But he asked for permission to study a while longer before he began his duties. He went to the University of Padua, in Italy again. This time, he chose to concentrate on medicine.

Learning to be a doctor in the 1500s was very different from today. Anatomy was not well understood. Anything that involved cutting, including surgery, was a barber's job. Medical practice was full of superstition. Astrology was often a part of treatment. Doctors would make medicines from strange ingredients. Some of these ingredients included ground animal horns and gemstones. These were usually mixed with plenty of sugar. Copernicus's notebooks were full of such recipes. Some of his notes were for cosmetics— dyes and ways to remove unwanted hair—rather than for medicines.[22] After one recipe for a medicine, Copernicus wrote, "If God wills, it will help."[23]

Copernicus finished his studies abroad with a degree from the University of Ferrara, in Italy. He probably chose Ferrara because it charged low fees. This could be important to a student, because he was also expected to give gifts to his professors. At Ferrara, the tests were also easier.[24]

When Copernicus finished his education, he was thirty years old. He returned to Poland expecting to start his job as a canon at Frombork, a town in Warmia, a historical region in northern Poland. Nicolaus would not have to become a priest to do his job as a canon. His duties would involve keeping in touch with people and leading daily prayers, but he would not say Mass.

Bishop Lukasz Watzelrode must have recognized that a bright young man like his nephew could be useful. Instead of allowing Copernicus to go directly to his position at Frombork, the bishop asked him to come to his residence at Lidzbark. For the next several years, Copernicus would serve his uncle as personal physician and secretary. Copernicus would sit close by his uncle at dinner. He would also travel with him.

Bishop Watzelrode's opinions were highly respected. His advice was often sought for political decisions.[25] Through him, Copernicus would meet kings and queens. He would also begin his dealings with the Teutonic Knights.[26]

Copernicus had a busy but comfortable position. Astronomy did not have to be a part of his life anymore. But throughout his student years, he had become fascinated by it. The skies over Warmia were often covered by clouds and fog, however. This made observations difficult. Copernicus himself called Warmia "the remote corner of the earth where I live."[27] He envied astronomers in ancient Egypt their clear skies, because "they were favored by a clearer atmosphere at a place, where the Nile—so they say—does not give out vapours as the Vistula does among us."[28]

When his day's duties were done, Copernicus would spend his nights studying the heavens. And as he studied, he began to realize that many of the things he was observing did not make sense.

Chapter 3

A RADICAL THEORY

When Copernicus studied astronomy, he had learned from books that had been written over a thousand years before. Most of these books were written by ancient Greek philosophers and scientists. These scientists had observed the sun, the moon, the stars, and the planets. They had noticed repeating patterns in their observations. From these patterns, they formed theories about how the (then known) universe was put together. The theories that best explained the patterns and repetitions were passed down through the centuries.

Around 400 B.C., a Greek philosopher named Eudoxus had first proposed that everything we could see in the sky was set in spheres. Eudoxus had studied with a famous teacher, the philosopher Plato. Plato often taught using stories and myths. One of his stories told of a man who saw the machinery that made the universe move. The planets were set in bowls that spun on a giant spindle. Eudoxus copied Plato's idea, but made the bowls into spheres instead. Earth rested at the very center of all the spheres that made up the universe.[1]

About fifty years later, Aristotle (384–322 B.C.), another Greek philosopher, developed this idea further. He said that all the heavenly bodies were indeed set in spheres with Earth at their center. All orbits had to be circles, because circles were perfect, and the universe must be perfect. But scientists had been observing and recording the movements of the planets for centuries. Circular orbits could not explain what they observed. They also could not help people predict where a planet would be in a month or a year. This was very important to astrologers, who used such information to predict the future. To explain any contradictions, Aristotle proposed a system of more than fifty spheres. Each one rested inside another, with no space between them. Each planet occupied its own formation of spheres, moving from one to another.[2]

Claudius Ptolemy was a famed Greek mathematician who lived in Egypt during the second century A.D.

His writings included a catalog of over one thousand stars, and an explanation of all the spheres of the planets. He compiled a book that charted the positions of heavenly bodies. This book also explained how to calculate how far north or south of the equator you were, using the stars. Later, Ptolemy's book was discovered by Arab scholars and traders. They appreciated its value for navigation. In 800 A.D., it was translated into Arabic, and became known as the Almagest. Over three hundred years later, it was translated into Latin, the language of European scholars.[3]

For centuries, people in Western Europe did not travel much. But by the Middle Ages, that was beginning to change. Merchants and explorers were traveling farther and farther. They needed help navigating during these voyages. Ptolemy's Almagest was still in use. Newer books used to chart the stars, such as the Alfonsine Tables, would eventually be compiled as well.

Copernicus's professors had taught the geocentric theory of the universe. Since Copernicus had studied Greek, he was able to read some of the works of the ancient Greeks in their original language. The more he read and observed, the more he realized that the geocentric theory might not be correct.

During Copernicus's lifetime, astronomers kept increasing the number of spheres in Aristotle's model. These additional spheres were needed to explain all the odd movements of the planets. Copernicus felt that Nature would tend toward the simplest motions. He disagreed with the complicated maze of circles that others proposed. He said of these theories:

> But they are in exactly the same fix as someone taking from different places hands, feet, head, and the other limbs—shaped very beautifully but not with reference to one body and without correspondence to one another—so that such parts made up a monster rather than a man.[4]

Copernicus compiled data from ancient astronomers and made his own observations. With an open mind, he looked for a model that would explain what he observed.

From his reading of ancient texts, Copernicus knew that not all Greek scientists agreed with the geocentric theory. Some believed that the earth, the sun, and the rest of the heavenly bodies revolved around a fire at the center of the universe. Others taught that Mercury and Venus went around the sun, but the sun and the rest of the planets circled Earth. And at least one man—Aristarchus of Samos, who lived around 350 B.C.—wrote that Earth and its fellow planets orbited the sun. Aristarchus also taught that the stars did not move and that they were very far away—much farther than Aristotle believed.[5]

By the second century, Ptolemy had recognized that the movements of the stars and planets were not uniform. So his model proposed that the earth existed at a small distance from the center of the universe. At an equal distance from the center, but in the opposite direction from Earth, was something called an equant. An equant is a kind of balancing point. It was around this point that the planets supposedly revolved.

Ptolemy's model kept the earth in the center of the universe. It also kept the earth stationary, with the sun and other planets spinning around it. But there were still problems with it. First, it did not keep the planets moving at a uniform speed, which violated Aristotle's rules of celestial motion. This would later worry many philosophers. It also failed to explain the distance between planets or how large their orbits were. These were questions that interested many people, including Copernicus.

Doing his best under the cloudy skies, Copernicus observed the planets. He used whatever instruments he could make or obtain. Copernicus had an astrolabe, a tool sea captains used to calculate latitude from the stars. He also had a triquetrum made of three lengths of pine. Tycho Brahe (1546–1601), the Danish astronomer, later came into possession of this tool. Tycho was impressed that such accurate observations could be made with such a crude instrument.[6]

Copernicus studied lunar and solar eclipses and the passage of planets in front of certain stars. He tried to find a pattern that would predict when these events would occur. He could then determine the sizes of the planets' orbits. He hoped that this would lead him to an accurate model of the universe.

The answer that revealed itself from all of Copernicus's calculations was revolutionary. It went so much against what people believed, Copernicus hesitated to tell anyone about it. He did find a model that explained many of the motions of the stars. But Copernicus's theory transferred the earth from its special place at the center of the universe. It made Earth just another planet, like Mars or Mercury, circling a common center. And that center was the sun.

That was not the only revolutionary thing about Copernicus's theory. In the old, accepted system, the earth stood still as the universe whirled around it. Day and night happened because the sun circled the earth every twenty-four hours. The only way to explain day and night under Copernicus's theory was for the earth to rotate while the sun stood still.

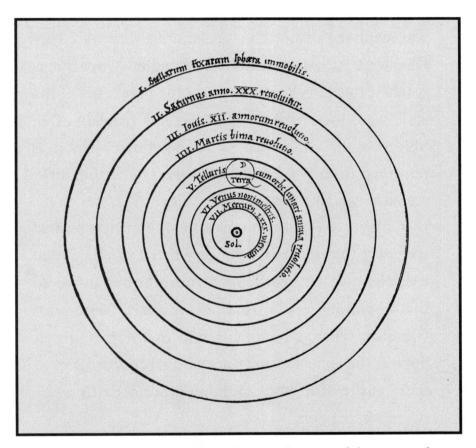

A page from Copernicus's On the Revolutions of the Heavenly Spheres, *first published in 1543. It shows a diagram of the solar system with seven planets in circular orbits and Earth as number V, Telluris.*

Copernicus still believed that the stars were points of light set in their own spheres. But they did not circle the earth. It appeared this way only because the earth was revolving around the sun. And the stars were very far away, as Aristarchus had taught. Copernicus reached this conclusion because the parallaxes of the stars were too small to measure. The parallax of an object is the difference in its position when it is observed from two separate places. The farther away something is, the smaller its parallax.

Copernicus had responses for the criticisms that were sure to come. For instance, when it was suggested to Ptolemy that the earth might move, he had answered that a spinning world would break apart.[7] With great common sense, Copernicus said that something as huge as the sphere of the stars would break apart even more easily, if it were spinning around Earth every twenty-four hours![8]

Besides offering proof that the stars were very far away, Copernicus also determined the order the planets were in, and approximately how far away from the sun they were. Some ancient Greek philosophers had placed Mercury and Venus between the sun and the earth. Others had placed them on the next spheres beyond the earth and the sun.[9]

Copernicus's heliocentric model finally explained the proper order and spacing of the planets. This was something Ptolemy's model was unable to do. With the sun at the center of the universe, the size of each planet's orbit revealed its distance. Since Mercury and Venus have orbits smaller than Earth's, they must be closer to the sun. Copernicus correctly concluded that Earth was the third planet away from the sun, between Venus and Mars. After Mars came Jupiter and Saturn, then the stars.[10] (Before the invention of the telescope, scientists were not aware of the planets Uranus, Neptune, or the dwarf planet Pluto.)

Another issue that had puzzled astronomers for centuries was the path of Mars. For a while, the planet appears to move forward in the sky. Then it seems to stop and move backward. Its motion sometimes traces a Z shape through the heavens. Other times, it is more like a loop. Copernicus's model finally explained why Mars appears to move this way.

When Earth is behind Mars in its orbit, Mars appears to move forward. But eventually, Earth's orbit overtakes that of Mars. When this happens, Mars appears to fall backward. This is called retrograde motion. It is much like being in a race. If someone runs ahead of you, he looks like he is moving forward. But if you pass him and look back at him over your shoulder, he appears to be falling backward. This is what happens when Earth passes Mars. All of this was impossible to explain in a geocentric model.

There were still things Copernicus could not explain. He still had trouble predicting where a planet would be using circular orbits. So he proposed little circles that spun around the perimeter of the planets' orbits. These little circles were called epicycles. Ptolemy had also used epicycles to explain irregularities in his model. Many years later, Johannes Kepler (1571–1630) showed that the orbits of the planets are ellipses, not circles. Only then could these motions be explained without epicycles.

Copernicus did not develop his heliocentric theoquickly. He worked on it gradually, all his life. Every day, he would make more observations. He would perform calculations and write down his conclusions. And this was not even his real job—astronomy was what he did in his spare time. Copernicus was one of the few medieval or Renaissance astronomers who did not make his living as an astrologer.[11] In fact, it appears Copernicus did not believe all that much in astrology. When people claimed that the world would end on February 11, 1524, because of a conjunction of the planets, Copernicus did not even dignify the rumor with a comment.[12]

At night, Copernicus would continue to observe the stars and planets. But during the day, the official duties he performed were very different and had little to do with the stars.

THE MULTITALENTED CANON

When King Sigismund of Poland got married, he invited Bishop Watzelrode to the wedding. Some accounts say that Copernicus accompanied his uncle to the event.[1] Others say he did not.[2] In any case, on his way back to Lidzbark Castle, the bishop fell ill. Copernicus was unable to help him. The bishop eventually died on March 29, 1512.

After the death of his uncle, Copernicus moved to Frombork and took up his duties as a canon. Bishop Watzelrode had also helped Copernicus's brother, Andrew, get an appointment as a canon at Frombork. The brothers lived there together until Andrew became ill in 1514. His illness may have been leprosy.

The medieval medicines made of ground-up jewels could not cure him. After he got sick, he returned to the warmer climate of Italy. He died in Rome, around 1518.[3]

Like the other canons, Copernicus had a comfortable home outside the city walls. He was permitted two servants and three horses.[4] At Frombork, Copernicus set up an observatory for himself. This may have been in a tower in the city walls—perhaps the one in the northwest corner. Today this tower is called Copernicus Tower. But Copernicus may have kept his real observatory in the yard outside his house.[5]

Copernicus earned a reputation for being organized, capable, and fair. The Chapter of Warmia, the organization that governed the canons, gave him many responsibilities. For several years, he served as administrator of the estates in Warmia. This meant that he would travel about the region, accompanied by his page, Hieronym, and his servant, Wojciech Szebulski.[6] He would keep track of the people occupying each farm. When a tenant died or a farm was abandoned, Copernicus took care of finding a new tenant. He would distribute the livestock and goods needed to get the farm working.[7] For a while, Copernicus was also the chancellor of the Chapter. In this capacity, he kept the account books and wrote official letters.[8]

Some of his positions and duties required Copernicus to spend several years in the city of Olsztyn instead of at Frombork.[9] Olsztyn was the headquarters of his chapter. He set up an observatory there, just as he had at Frombork. On a wall of Olsztyn Castle, the faint outlines of a grid drawn by Copernicus can still be seen. A mirror would have been positioned nearby, to reflect the sun's rays onto the wall. This worked like a sundial for solar observations. The grid on the wall of Olsztyn Castle is the only known surviving astronomical tool used by Copernicus himself.[10] The stairs from the room that was probably his office at Olsztyn led up to a little tower. Copernicus may also have used this tower to observe the skies.[11]

At this point, Copernicus had never published a book on astronomy. In fact, his only published book was a translation of some Greek love letters.[12] When this book was printed in 1509, it was the first translation from Greek to Latin ever published in Poland.[13] Even so, Copernicus's reputation as a student of the heavens was well known.

In the early 1500s, it was recognized that there was a problem with the calendar. The calendar in use had been instituted by the Roman Emperor Julius Caesar in 46 B.C. A year was 365 days long—366 every fourth, or leap, year. But this was still about eleven minutes longer than it takes for the earth to complete its orbit of the sun.[14] Eleven minutes may not sound like much, but over the centuries, those minutes added up.[15] By the 1500s, the date that was celebrated as the first day of spring no longer coincided with the vernal equinox. The vernal equinox occurs when the center of the sun is directly over the equator. Pope Leo X wanted to consult with the best astronomers of the time to decide what to do. One of the men he contacted was Copernicus. Copernicus replied with some ideas for reforming the calendar. But he advised the pope to do nothing until astronomers could make more observations.[16] Finally, in 1582, Pope Gregory XIII authorized the changes necessary to correct the calendar.[17]

Many men at the dawn of the Renaissance had numerous talents. One was Leonardo da Vinci. He was an Italian who lived around the same time as Copernicus. He was a painter and an inventor, among other things. Michelangelo was a painter and sculptor. Erasmus, Machiavelli, and Thomas More were philosophers and writers.[18] Today, we still call people with many skills "Renaissance men." Copernicus certainly would qualify as a "Renaissance man." He had many interests in addition to astronomy. Among them were medicine, economics, diplomacy, map-making, painting, and poetry.

One cause Copernicus got involved with was money: not making or spending it, but deciding how much it was worth. Poland was a huge kingdom, but it was not really unified. Some areas had sworn allegiance to the king of Poland just to get protection from the Teutonic Knights. These lands wanted to continue to use their own kind of money, not Polish coins. This was confusing for trade purposes.

Besides the different kinds of money in the kingdom, there was also a problem with what the coins were made of. The original coins were made of nearly pure silver, but mints around the country would melt down the coins. They would then mix the melted silver with cheaper metals and stamp new coins. Because these coins contained less silver, they were not as valuable. Copernicus recognized that money should be worth as much as it was supposed to be worth. With so many cheapened coins in circulation, the kingdom was less wealthy than it believed. This could be disastrous for business and trade.

In his "Treatise on the Method of Minting Money," Copernicus warned people about the cheapened coins. He said that these coins were as dangerous to the country as a war or a bad harvest.[19] Copernicus hoped the king would collect all the bad coins and exchange them for new silver coins. He also recommended a centralized mint. Most of his suggestions were ignored or not adopted until much later.[20]

The value of bread also interested Copernicus. When bakers in Warmia began charging exorbitant prices for their bread, Copernicus set up a plan to make the price more fair. He suggested that a loaf of bread ought to cost as much as the grain used to make it.

Copernicus had served his uncle well as both a doctor and a secretary. When the new bishop was appointed, he had his own staff, but he kept Copernicus on as his personal physician. In fact, Copernicus was the official doctor to four consecutive bishops of Warmia.[21] The fourth, Bishop Dantiscus, did not get along with Copernicus. He would often challenge and antagonize him. But he still wanted Copernicus as his physician.[22]

Copernicus was even respected by his enemies. When the Grand Master of the Teutonic Knights became ill, the doctor summoned was none other than Copernicus.[23] Copernicus also offered to treat the peasants of Warmia, free of charge.[24] He was especially busy when epidemics of plague and cholera swept through the area in 1519.[25] In some paintings of Copernicus, he is shown holding a lily of the valley. In medieval times, this flower was a symbol of the medical profession.[26]

Copernicus also continued to work as a diplomat. Many times, he helped negotiate with the Teutonic Knights. Even in times of conflict, the Knights would often write letters granting him safe passage through their lands.[27] But when he had to, Copernicus was not afraid to fight. When necessary, he would organize men to battle the Knights in defense of their property. Copernicus himself lost his house outside Frombork's city walls when the Teutonic Knights swept through the area in 1520, burning and looting.[28]

The Teutonic Knights were also very interested in one of Copernicus's projects. Copernicus had drawn up the first accurate map of Warmia. This map would have been very useful to the Knights. One canon at Frombork was a spy for the Teutonic Knights. He sent several letters back to his superiors, describing his unsuccessful attempts to steal the map. In one letter, he reports that he "searched all the rooms of doctor Nicholas," but that Copernicus must have taken "the map with him or locked it in a coffer."[29] Copernicus and a classmate from Krakow, Bernard Wapowski, are also supposed to have worked together on a map of the entire kingdom of Poland.[30]

Maps were not all that Copernicus could draw. On a clock at Strasbourg Cathedral, there is a painting of

Copernicus that is supposed to be a copy of a self-portrait.[31] Unfortunately, the original has been lost.

As a true Renaissance man, Copernicus had many talents. But the project he dedicated his life to was his heliocentric model of the solar system. As early as 1507, he sketched out his theory in an essay he called "Commentary on the Hypothesis of the Movement of Celestial Orbs."

His theory, which proposed that the earth rotated on its own axis while also revolving around the sun, was complicated. But it was much less complicated than the eighty-sphere systems being taught in universities. As Copernicus described it:

> Mercury thus moves along seven circles in all, Venus along five, the earth along three, and the moon around the earth along four. And finally, Mars, Jupiter and Saturn each move along five circles. And so thirty-four circles are sufficient to explain the structure of the world and the entire dance of the planets.[32]

The twenty-page manuscript was never published in his lifetime, but Copernicus wrote out several copies by hand. He sent them to his friends and interested scientists. Tycho Brahe also owned a copy of the "Commentary."[33] Word of the theory spread around Europe.

But for such a revolutionary theory to be accepted, Copernicus would have to offer mathematical details. And this is exactly what he worked on all his life: a book that not only proposed his theory, but also showed how it worked. It was a book only a mathematician would be able to read and understand completely.

Chapter 5

LABOR OF A LIFETIME

Copernicus probably started writing the book explaining his heliocentric theory around 1515, maybe even earlier. He finished most of the writing around 1530. But for years afterward he continued to revise his work.

The manuscript was made up of six "books," or chapters. In them, Copernicus summarized the ancient theories of the universe. He then described his heliocentric model and proposed three motions for the earth. First, the earth completely circles the sun once a year. This is called the annual revolution of the earth. It produces the regular change of seasons each year. Second, the earth rotates (spins in place) from west to east. It takes one full day for the earth to turn around completely. This turning is what produces day and night. Because we do not sense the earth spinning, it appears that the sun and stars move from east to west. Only the North Star does not change its position. This star, called Polaris, always seems to appear directly above the North Pole.

The constant position of the North Star meant that there had to be another motion for the earth. This motion had to cancel out Earth's annual revolution in order to explain why the North Star does not appear to move. So Copernicus proposed a third motion. This motion was an additional rotation for the earth, on its axis. (Much like a spinning top, the earth moves in more than one direction at a time.) Earth's axis is an imaginary line that divides the planet in half. This third motion is in the opposite direction of Earth's yearly revolution around the sun.

However, based on the observations of ancient scientists, Copernicus knew that this third motion took slightly less than a year to complete. So it did not entirely cancel out the revolution around the sun. This meant that the North Star would shift over a long period of time. A different star could then assume the position of the North Star. However, this assumption of position takes so long for this to happen that the casual observer will never notice it. Astronomers refer to this shifting as the Precession of the Equinoxes. Copernicus had mistakenly calculated that the Precession would take 53,000 years. Today, we know that this cycle actually takes about 26,000 years to complete. So in 13,000 years, the star Vega will become the North Star. Another 13,000 years after that, Polaris will once again be the North Star.[1]

Throughout his book, Copernicus diagrams how his heliocentric theory can explain many of the inconsistencies in the old geocentric theory. He also provides star charts, as well as instructions for making astronomical instruments and directions for calculating eclipses. Much of the manuscript, however, consists of mathematical calculations.

Copernicus had distributed handwritten copies of his little "Commentary" to his friends. But he kept his longer work to himself. He later explained that he was afraid people would consider his ideas ridiculous and mock them.[2]

And Copernicus was right. People did make fun of his ideas, even before he published his book. Wilhelm Gnapheus wrote a play called Morosophus, about a wise man with absurd ideas. One of the characters is a foolish astronomer who insists that the earth circles the sun. This character is unmistakably based on Copernicus.[3]

The leaders of the growing Protestant movement also ridiculed Copernicus. John Calvin said: "Who would dare place Copernicus's authority higher than Holy Scripture?"[4] Martin Luther, the founder of the Protestant reform movement, derided that:

> [The] new astrologer who would prove that the earth moves, not the sky and the firmament, sun and moon. . . . The fool would like to reverse the whole art of astronomy! But it says in the Holy Writ that Joshua bade the sun stand still, not the earth![5]

A Protestant scholar and teacher named Philip Melanchthon wrote:

> Our eyes are witnesses to the fact that the heavens do rotate once every twenty-four hours. But a certain man, either out of a love of novelty, or perhaps in order to display his inventiveness, has come to the conclusion that the earth moves, and he proclaims that neither the Sun nor the heavenly spheres move. . . . It is a lack of honesty and decency to assert such things in public.[6]

Ironically, it was a young student of Melanchthon who convinced Copernicus to offer his full theory to the world. This young man's name was George Joachim Lauchen, but he called himself Rheticus, after the Latin name for the region of Austria where he had grown up.[7] In May 1539, he arrived in Frombork, hoping to meet Copernicus. With him he brought gifts for the astronomer—valuable editions of mathematical and scientific books by Regiomontanus, Ptolemy, and Euclid.[8] Rheticus had heard about Copernicus's heliocentric theory, and wanted to know more about it.

Rheticus spent the next two years by Copernicus's side. During that time, he convinced the elderly astronomer to publish the book he had been working on for almost his whole life. As Copernicus acknowledged in the introduction he now added to his book, "my friends made me change my course in spite of my long-continued hesitation and even resistance."[9]

Besides Rheticus, those friends included Tiedemann Giese and Cardinal Nicholas Schonberg. Schonberg had been encouraging Copernicus to publish his ideas for years, because the present pope, Paul III, had a scholarly reputation. In fact, Copernicus dedicated his book to Pope Paul III.[10] The publication of Copernicus's manuscript would give "the results of my nocturnal study to the light." It would bring "to light a work which I had kept hidden among my things for not merely nine years, but for about four times nine years."[11]

Before Copernicus's own book was published, Rheticus wrote and published a brief summary of it. He called his book *First Narrative*. Like Copernicus's earlier "Commentary," it introduced his heliocentric theory. But it was a version for ordinary readers, who would not be able to follow the complex mathematics in Copernicus's book. In his book, Rheticus never calls Copernicus by name. He just refers to him as his teacher.[12] Rheticus is also supposed to have written a biography of his mentor, but if it ever existed, it has since been lost.[13]

Rheticus found a publisher for Copernicus's book in the German city of Nuremberg. The young man brought the manuscript to an editor, Andreas Osiander. The manuscript did not yet have a title.[14] Osiander assigned it a Latin title that translates to *On the Revolutions of the Heavenly Spheres.*

Osiander contacted Copernicus, suggesting that the astronomer call his idea a hypothesis. A hypothesis is an idea that may or may not be true. But Copernicus refused to do as the editor asked. He believed that his new model of the solar system was much more than a hypothesis. He believed that it was truth, with mathematical support.

Instead of honoring the author's wishes, Osiander wrote an additional preface for the book. Editors do sometimes add a brief introduction, but it is usually labeled "Editor's Note." Osiander's preface was not labeled, however. In the first edition of the book, it looked like part of Copernicus's work. And in the books's preface, Osiander called the theory presented in the book a hypothesis. The preface implied that Copernicus himself did not really believe that his heliocentric theory was true.[15]

Almost immediately, Tiedemann Giese began to publicly protest Osiander's preface to his friend's book.[16] But for years, readers would accept those contradictory paragraphs about a hypothesis as Copernicus's own work.

On the Revolutions of the Heavenly Spheres was published in March 1543. The only payment Copernicus was expecting for his life's work was a few free copies of the book.[17] Then, while he was waiting to see the finished volume, the seventy-year-old astronomer suffered a stroke. He lay in bed in his room at Frombork, his right side paralyzed. As the days went on, his condition grew worse. He lapsed into a coma.[18]

On May 24, 1543, a copy of *On the Revolutions of the Heavenly Spheres* finally arrived at Frombork. Copernicus was barely alive. The book was placed in his hands. Copernicus's dear friend, Tiedemann Giese, was there. Giese said in a letter he wrote to Rheticus two months later that, "he saw his completed work only at his last breath upon the day that he died."[19]

Before his death, Copernicus had recommended that a young relative, Jan Loitz, should replace him as canon at Frombork. After Copernicus's passing, Loitz was appointed to the post.[20] In his will, Copernicus left his sister Catherine's children and grandchildren some money.[21] He donated his small but impressive collection of scientific books to his chapter's library. When the Swedish army attacked Poland the following century, it had the valuable books sent back to Sweden.[22]

For years, the manuscript of *On the Revolutions of the Heavenly Spheres* that Rheticus had taken to Nuremberg was presumed lost. But in the 1800s, it was discovered in the library of a nobleman in Prague.[23]

Nicolaus Copernicus was buried beneath the floor of Frombork Cathedral—a place of honor. But subsequent burials and the devastation of the many wars that have plagued Poland have erased any hint of exactly where his body may have lain. The body may even have disappeared when Swedish soldiers desecrated the cathedral's tombs in the seventeenth century. Frombork also suffered great destruction during the Second World War.[24] A plaque in the renovated cathedral now commemorates Frombork's most famous canon.

Chapter 6

THE LEGACY OF COPERNICUS

Copernicus died at a time when his heliocentric model of the universe was just beginning to gain recognition. Now that it was available in a book, more people would have access to it. Only scientists would be likely to understand its diagrams and math. But anyone who could read could grasp the main ideas from the first few chapters.

These ideas were not immediately accepted, but Copernicus's theory found an application fairly soon. An almanac, charting the positions of the planets day by day, was calculated using his system. When astronomers observed a conjunction of the planets Jupiter and Saturn in 1563, they found Copernican tables more accurate than those based on Ptolemy's work.[1]

Astrologers who wanted to chart more accurate horoscopes also used the research of Copernicus.[2] One famous horoscope that was cast using Copernicus's data was Martin Luther's.[3]

Young Rheticus should have been his mentor's first real advocate, but he began to pursue interests in chemistry and medicine more than astronomy. The ideas he did have about astronomy became more like astrology. Rheticus spent the rest of his life moving about Europe. Some people, including the astronomer Johannes Kepler, said that Rheticus went mad. They blamed his insanity on his struggles to understand the retrograde motion of Mars.[4]

One of the earliest and most vocal supporters of Copernicus's theory was Giordano Bruno (1548–1600). But much like Rheticus, Bruno turned out to be a less-than-credible spokesman. He had been a monk, but left his order to become a traveling philosopher. He was not an astronomer, and his ideas went far beyond those of Copernicus. In his public speeches, Bruno described a solar system in which Earth and its fellow planets revolved around a sun that was not the center of the universe. He also said there might be other solar systems with inhabited planets.[5] He spent several years at the court of Queen Elizabeth I in England, introducing the British to the idea of a heliocentric solar system.[6] By 1576, parts of *On the Revolutions of the Heavenly Spheres* had been translated into English.[7]

By this time, however, Bruno was not quite free to speak as he wished. New ideas were spreading through Europe. Some of these ideas challenged centuries of religious tradition. Men like John Calvin and Martin Luther even founded new religions. This made the Catholic Church more fearful of new ideas. The Church set up a court called the Inquisition. The Inquisition tried people for heresy—beliefs that challenged church teachings. People whose ideas were found objectionable could be pressured to say they were mistaken. Those who refused could be imprisoned, tortured, or even killed. Bruno was among those eventually put to death for his unusual beliefs.

Meanwhile, real astronomers began taking Copernicus's theory seriously. Among them was Tycho Brahe of Denmark, who came into possession of Copernicus's triquetrum. The King of Denmark gave Tycho an island, where he built the famous observatory of Uraniborg. He worked there until a later king banished him, and then he moved to Prague. Tycho was one of the last major astronomers to work without the benefit of a telescope.[8] He recorded many observations of the stars and planets over the years. Tycho disagreed with Copernicus's theory, however. According to Tycho, Mercury, Venus, Mars, Jupiter, and Saturn did revolve around the sun. But Earth was the center of Tycho's universe. The sun and its family of planets, along with the stars, orbited the earth.[9]

In Prague, Tycho had an assistant named Johannes Kepler. Kepler eventually inherited Tycho's notebooks and carried on his work in astronomy. But Kepler did not agree with his mentor's model of the universe. He wrote: "I base all my astronomy on Copernicus's hypotheses, on Tycho de Brahe's observations and finally on the magnetic philosophy of the Englishman William Gilbert."[10]

Kepler combined the data and theories from these three sources. He came to the conclusion that Earth and its fellow planets do orbit the sun, but not exactly in circles. The orbits Kepler proposed were slightly stretched circles called ellipses. With this proposal, some of the few inconsistencies in Copernicus's model began to disappear. Stripped of circles and crystal spheres, this universe no longer resembled the one ancient thinkers imagined. But these new theories were describing the world more and more accurately.

Around this same time, an Italian astronomer named Galileo Galilei (1564–1642) was intrigued by a novelty he had heard about. Glass lenses, properly arranged in a tube, could make distant objects appear closer. Galileo experimented with lenses until he developed a working telescope. When he turned this new invention toward the moon, Galileo saw something incredible. He saw that the moon was not a smooth, perfect body, as the ancient astronomers had taught. It was covered with mountains and craters. He also saw the planet Venus go through phases, like the moon. According to Copernicus's theory, Venus would have to go through phases. But before the invention of the telescope, it had been impossible to see them.[11] Galileo also saw that Jupiter had at least four moons circling it. This last discovery proved that not everything in the universe revolved around the earth.

Galileo had heard of Kepler's work and began a correspondence with him. In one letter, he wrote:

> I have for many years been a partisan of the Copernican view because it reveals to me the causes of many natural phenomena that are entirely incomprehensible in the light of the generally accepted hypotheses. To refute the latter I have collected many proofs, but I do not publish them, because I am deterred by the fate of our teacher Copernicus who, although he had won immortal fame with a few, was ridiculed and condemned by countless people (for very great is the number of the stupid).[12]

Despite these fears, Galileo eventually began to promote Copernicus's heliocentric theory, which made more sense the more he observed.

By the time of the early seventeenth century, the Inquisition was no longer the only threat to new ideas. The Catholic Church began to publish a list of books, called the Index, which good Catholics were not allowed to read. These books were supposed to contain heretical ideas. Despite its dedication to a pope, Copernicus's *On the Revolutions of the Heavenly Spheres* was among the books placed on the Index. Pope Urban VII actually said that Copernicus's book was more dangerous than the growing Protestant movement.[13] In 1616, the group of churchmen compiling the Index stated:

> the false teaching of the Pythagoreans, which is wholly alien to Holy Scripture, about the motion of the Earth and the immobility of the Sun, which teaching is voiced by Nicolaus Copernicus in his *The Revolutions of the Heavenly Bodies* . . . has already become widespread and has been accepted by many. . . . Accordingly, in order that teaching of this type should not disseminate further to the detriment of the Catholic truth, it has been deemed proper necessarily to suspend the aforementioned works.[14]

On the Revolutions of the Heavenly Spheres was placed on the Index. In 1620, the Catholic Church stated that the earth was not a planet and that it did not move.[15] Galileo dutifully paged through his copy of *On the Revolutions* and noted the ten specific corrections required by the Index. But he crossed the heretical lines out in very light pencil, so he could still read them.[16]

By the 1630s, the Inquisition had already questioned Galileo on his beliefs about the motion of the earth and its place in the universe. They had forbidden him to teach or write that the Copernican theory was true. But he could not remain silent.

Now an old man, Galileo wrote a book entitled *Dialogue Concerning the Two Chief World Systems*. In it, he invented a conversation between three scholars. One scholar supported a geocentric model of the universe. Another, with stronger and more logical ideas, argued in favor of a heliocentric system. The third scholar judged the arguments of the other two. Galileo did not directly choose one side over the other. He left the final conclusion up to the reader.[17]

Once again, Galileo was summoned to a trial before the Inquisition. He argued that his book taught about the Copernican theory but did not advocate it. Nevertheless, Galileo was found guilty of disobeying the court's earlier order. Galileo spent the final years of his life under house arrest—all for agreeing with Copernicus. Galileo's *Dialogue* was also added to the Index of forbidden books.

Like Galileo, professors in the Catholic universities of Europe could teach about the heliocentric model as a hypothesis. But they could not argue that the hypothesis might be true.[18] It would be almost two hundred years before the church removed *On the Revolutions of the Heavenly Spheres* from the Index. By that time, of course, most Catholics had embraced the heliocentric model. As philosopher and mathematician Blaise Pascal understood in the seventeenth century, "It is not the decree of Rome which will prove that the earth remains at rest; and, if we had constant observations to prove that it does turn, not all the people in the world could stop it from turning, nor could they stop themselves from turning with it."[19]

The work of Nicolaus Copernicus, Brahe, Kepler, and Galileo helped eliminate the idea of crystal spheres that made up the heavens. But if the stars and planets were not set in spheres, what held them in place? Sir Isaac Newton answered that question in 1666. That year, Newton proposed the laws of gravity. The heliocentric theory of the solar system now conformed to

This statue of Copernicus was first unveiled in 1853. Today, it stands near the Old Town Hall in Torun, the astronomer's birthplace.

all that was being learned about the workings of the universe. The geocentric theory no longer did.

During Copernicus's youth, Europeans had discovered the continent of North America. (In fact, Copernicus mentions America in *On the Revolutions*, stating somewhat incorrectly that it was named after the sea captain who discovered it.[20]) Two hundred fifty years later, Americans were discussing the astronomer's theory. A leading Puritan minister, Cotton Mather, considered whether the heliocentric theory should be accepted. In 1721, Mather wrote: "The Copernican hypothesis is now generally preferred," and "there is no objection against the motion of the earth."[21]

At last, in 1820, the Catholic Church removed *On the Revolutions of the Heavenly Spheres* from the Index.[22] The ideas in Copernicus's life's work were not threats to religion. They were one man's attempt, using the crude and limited resources of his day, to explain how the universe really worked.

The Renaissance was full of men and women bursting with exciting new thoughts and ideas. They expressed these ideas in literature and philosophy. They expressed them in painting and sculpture. They expressed them in architecture and music. And they also expressed them through science.

Most Renaissance thinkers celebrated humanity as the most special creation in the universe. In one way, Copernicus made mankind a little less special. He shifted man's home from the center of all things. Now it was just an ordinary point on a circle in the midst of other circles. As the nineteenth-century German poet Goethe realized:

> Of all discoveries and opinions, none may have exerted a greater effect on the human spirit than the doctrine of Copernicus. The world had scarcely become known as round and complete in itself when it was asked to waive the tremendous privilege of being the center of the universe. Never, perhaps, was a greater demand made on mankind.[23]

CONTINUED REVOLUTIONS

T o Copernicus, a heliocentric solar system was not only mathematically correct, it was also elegant, beautiful, and appropriate:

At the middle of all things lies the sun. As the location of this luminary in the cosmos, that most beautiful temple, would there be any other place or any better place than the center, from which it can light up everything at the same time? Hence the sun is not inappropriately called by some the lamp of the universe, by others its mind, and by others its ruler.[1]

Some modern scholars have questioned, however, just how much contemporary thinkers shared Copernicus's enthusiasm for his work. Arthur Koestler, who wrote about the great minds of the Renaissance and the Reformation entitled *The Sleepwalkers,* stated that no one really read *On the Revolutions.* In his words, the book "was and is an all-time worst-seller."[2] More recently, a science historian named Owen Gingerich set out to disprove this idea. He traveled all around the world, seeking out copies of Copernicus's book in libraries and private collections.

Considering the way books were treated in Europe in the years following the Renaissance, it is amazing that original printings of the works of scientists like Copernicus could survive at all. Merchants bought up entire libraries—like Oxford University's in the mid-1500s—for incredibly low prices, just to tear the books apart. They would use the pages as wrapping; as scouring pads for household utensils; as material for shining their shoes; even as toilet paper![3]

In another example from the early 1600s, a nobleman's library was loaded onto a boat for shipment. The ship was attacked by pirates who were looking for fine Italian gold and jewels. They were so disgusted with what they found in the cargo hold, they simply tossed the entire collection of books into the sea.[4]

Amazingly, Gingerich was not only able to find many copies of *On the Revolutions*; he was often able to determine who had owned the book originally. Contrary to Koestler's assertion, most of the great thinkers of the age not only acquired copies of *On the Revolutions*, they actually used it as a sort of textbook. They wrote notes into the margins, commenting on science and philosophy and religion, and on observations they had made using the book. Sometimes even the mathematical formulae and geometrical diagrams had notes scribbled alongside.[5]

It is a testament to how widely valued *On the Revolutions* was that so many copies survived. Due largely to Gingerich's work, the original book has now been researched and cataloged better than any first-edition historical text except for the original Gutenberg Bible.[6]

The Growing Universe

As time passed, our understanding of the universe continued to grow. In 1781, more than fifty years after the death of Isaac Newton, the planet Uranus was discovered. After the discovery of Uranus, it was noticed that its orbit was irregular. It did not behave the way it was supposed to, at least not according to Newton's laws. Scientists believed that this meant there had to be another, more distant planet that was effecting the orbit of Uranus. This planet was first observed in 1846 and named Neptune.

Once again, the motions of Uranus and Neptune led scientists to believe there was yet another planet, still further away. The search was underway for this mystery planet, which was referred to as "Planet X." Finally, in 1930, astronomer Clyde Tombaugh discovered an object in the predicted location of Planet X, which was named Pluto. As it turned out, the calculations predicting the location of Planet X were made in error—Pluto's discovery was a happy accident. It was not Planet X. Besides, Pluto was too small to effect the motions of Uranus and Neptune. The search continued for Planet X, but it would never be found. We know today that there is no Planet X.[7]

Einstein

For nearly 300 years, Newton's laws had explained nearly all the motions of the universe. One of the rare exceptions was the planet Mercury. It took until the twentieth century, when Albert Einstein's General Theory of Relativity finally explained the motions of this tiny planet.

Newton's calculations had shown that the moon, the stars, and the planets are all attracted to each other. The strength of the attraction depended on the mass of the objects and the distance between them. This force of attraction is what he called the law of gravity. Newton's law of gravity tried to explain nature in a simple way—but nature was not quite so simple.

According to Albert Einstein's General Theory of Relativity, gravity would cause the fabric of space (and time) to curve (or warp). With this in mind, Einstein predicted that light would bend as it came near a body in space. Upon experimentation, scientists have found that Einstein's formulas correctly charted the orbit of Mercury. As the planet closest to the sun, Mercury's path is affected by the sun's warping of space.

More and more, century after century, the scientific view of our universe was evolving. By the mid-twentieth century, astronauts were taking test flights in space. In 1969, men walked on the surface of the moon. By the time of the twenty-first century, space probes were sending back images of the surface of Mars. Copernicus could have only dreamed of viewing such details!

Planet or not?

An interesting dilemma arose at this time. As we continued exploring our galaxy, we found other objects in the Kuiper Belt, just beyond Neptune. Then Eris was discovered beyond the Kuiper Belt. It was more fully studied in 2005 and found to be even larger than Pluto. Scientists began to debate if Eris was really a planet. The dilemma was this: If Eris was not a planet, than how could Pluto be a planet?

The possibility of discovering more bodies like Eris spurred the IAU (International Astronomical Union) to define what a planet was for the first time. By this definition, which was approved in August 2006, Pluto would no longer be considered a planet. It is now classified as a dwarf planet, along with Eris and Ceres.[8]

Nothing had changed about Pluto to cause this. It was people's understanding of the universe that had changed. Many people—including some scientists—were upset by the fact that we had "lost" a planet. There was a sentimental attachment to Pluto as a planet. This attachment can be seen as very similar to the one people once had for the idea that Earth was the center of the universe. As one scientist put it:

> The 16th century realization that the sun (not Earth!) is the center of our solar system, jarred perceptions and changed textbooks in revolutionary ways. Just as jarring to us now is the newly emerging view that our solar system . . . is still littered with very many distant planets, most of which are nothing like the familiar planets that orbit close to the sun, like Earth.
>
> In a real sense, we are seeing a new chapter unfold in the revolution that Copernicus wrought when he displaced the Earth from the center of everything.[9]

For over many centuries, it was widely accepted that the sun revolved around Earth. Copernicus proved that this idea was wrong. For over seventy years since its discovery, Pluto was thought to be a planet. Now this is no longer so. What other long-held belief might science prove untrue someday?

ACTIVITIES

Activity One: Retrograde Motion

Copernicus's heliocentric theory successfully explained one observational oddity that no other model could. This was the apparent retrograde motion in the orbit of the planet Mars. It was such a puzzle, it supposedly drove Rheticus insane. But retrograde motion is easy to observe today.

Ask an adult to drive you in a car onto a highway. When you pass a car that is moving slowly, look back. Both you and the car you passed are still moving forward. But to you, it looks like the slower car is moving backward.

The apparent retrograde motion of Mars is similar. When Earth is behind Mars in its orbit, it looks like Mars is moving forward. But because Earth is closer to the sun, it moves more rapidly around the sun than Mars does. As we on Earth catch up to Mars and pass it, it looks like Mars is moving backward—just like the slower car on the highway.

Activity Two: The Planets' Place in Space

Copernicus correctly determined the order of the planets out from the sun. He also determined the relative distance of each planet from the sun.

Today, astronomers measure distances in astronomical units. One astronomical unit, or AU, equals the distance from the earth to the sun. In astronomical units, the distances of the first six planets from the sun are:

(Remember, that in Copernicus's day, the planets Uranus and Neptune—and the dwarf planet, Pluto— had not yet been discovered.)

The star that is closest to Earth (other than the sun, of course) is Alpha Centauri. It is 271,395.36 astronomical units away!

Planet	Distance in AUs
Mercury	0.387
Venus	0.723
Earth	1
Mars	1.52
Jupiter	5.2
Saturn	9.54

Planet	Distance in AUs	Towel Pieces Away
Mercury	0.387	2
Venus	0.723	4
Earth	1	6
Mars	1.52	9
Jupiter	5.2	31
Saturn	9.54	57

You can make a human model of the solar system of Copernicus's day. You will need:

- 6 people
- A roll of paper towels
- A very long hallway or a large open space outdoors

For the purposes of this activity, six pieces of paper towel will represent an astronomical unit.

Have one person represent the sun at the center of the solar system. That person will hold the end of the roll of paper towels. The person representing Mercury will start walking away, unrolling the towels. Mercury

Planet	Distance in AUs	Paper Towel Pieces
Uranus	19.18	115
Neptune	30.07	180
Pluto (dwarf planet)	39.44	236

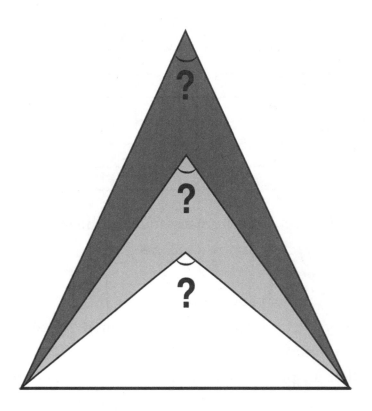

will stop two towel pieces away from the sun and hand the roll to Venus. Venus will stop four pieces from the sun and hand the roll to Earth. The remaining planets will go on, according to the table.

If you have enough space and would like to include the rest of the planets (and Pluto) in this activity, here is where they fit into the table:

How many paper towel pieces away from the sun would Alpha Centauri be?

Activity Three: Parallax

Copernicus concluded that the stars were very far away because he could not measure their parallax. Parallax is the angle formed when an object is observed from two different places. When the object is nearby, the angle is large. The farther away the object is, the smaller the angle becomes. When the object is very distant, such as a star, the angle of parallax is so small, you cannot measure it without sophisticated scientific instruments. Such instruments did not exist in the sixteenth century. To see how parallax works, you will need:

- Pins or tacks
- A piece of corkboard
- String or thread
- A protractor

Stick two pins in a straight line, about six inches apart, parallel to the bottom of the corkboard. Now locate the center of the line between the pins, and measure two inches up from that point. Stick a pin there. Wind the string or thread around the three pins to outline a triangle.

Measure four inches up from the center of the base line. Stick in another pin, and make another thread triangle.

Repeat this process with triangles six, eight, and ten inches high.

When you have finished making your triangles, take your protractor. Measure the angle at the tip of each progressively skinnier triangle. If there were observers standing at the two pins at the base line, and the object they were observing were the third pin at the tip of the triangle, the angle you measure would indicate its parallax.

What do you observe about the parallax angles of the triangles as they get taller?

How big (or small!) do you think the angle would be if the middle pin were a mile from the base line?

Activity Four: A Simple Astrolabe[1]

One of the tools Copernicus used was an astrolabe. It measures latitude. Early astrolabes were made of sturdier materials than string and plastic, and many were very precise, sophisticated instruments that did much more than measure latitude. Make your own simple astrolabe and use it to determine the latitude of the place where you live. For this you will need:

- Transparent tape
- A protractor
- A drinking straw
- A piece of string about one foot (.3 m) long
- A fishing sinker or other weight

Tape the drinking straw to the protractor as shown in the diagram. The straw should lie exactly across the center of the protractor and the 90-degree mark.

Thread the string through the center hole of the protractor and tie it around the straw. Tie the other end of the string to the weight. Let it hang freely.

You have an astrolabe!

To determine your latitude with the astrolabe, go outside on a clear night. Look in the northern sky for Polaris, the North Star. (To find Polaris, first locate the constellation Ursa Major or Big Dipper. Imagine a line joining the two stars on the edge of the "dipper," then extend the line about five times the distance between those two stars. At that point, you should see a relatively bright star: Polaris.)

Look for Polaris through the drinking straw part of your astrolabe. Hold it still until the string stops swinging. Then press the string against the protractor to hold it in the position it was freely hanging. The number of degrees you measure is your latitude. To be accurate, repeat the process a few times.

Later, look up your location in an atlas, that contains the latitude and longitude of locations around the world as well as many maps. How close to the figure in the atlas was the latitude you found with your astrolabe?

Even with a precise astrolabe like the one Copernicus used, you can see how hard it can be to take an accurate measurement. Copernicus made his observations night after night for many years, and carefully recorded them. Scientists today know that he made mistakes. It may take you a while to determine your correct latitude using your astrolabe.

CHRONOLOGY

1473—Nicolaus Kopernik is born on February 19 to Mikolaj and Barbara Kopernik of Torun, Poland.

1483—Mikolaj Kopernik dies.

1491–1495—Nicolaus attends University of Krakow.

1496—Nicolaus attends University of Bologna.

1497—Nicolaus and Domenico Maria da Novaro observe occultation of Aldebaran in Bologna on March 9.

1500—Nicolaus studies in Rome; assumes the name Copernicus.

1501—Copernicus attends University of Padua.

1503—Copernicus is awarded degree from University of Ferrara.

1504—Copernicus takes up his duties in Warmia with Lukasz Watzelrode at Lidzbark.

1507—Copernicus works on his "Commentary on the Hypothesis of the Movement of Celestial Orbs."

1510—Copernicus moves to Frombork.

1512—Bishop Lukasz Watzelrode dies on March 29.

1513—Copernicus is contacted by the Pope to help with the reform of the calendar.

1516–1520—Copernicus at Olsztyn.

1518—Andrew Kopernik dies in Rome.

1519–1520—Poland at war with the Teutonic Knights.

1521—Copernicus returns to Frombork.

1522–1529—Copernicus works on his essay on money.

1530—Copernicus finishes writing *On the Revolutions of the Heavenly Spheres*.

1539—Rheticus visits Copernicus.

1543—*On the Revolutions of the Heavenly Spheres* is published in March; Nicolaus Copernicus dies on May 24.

1546–1601—Life of Tycho Brahe.

1564–1642—Life of Galileo.

1571–1630—Life of Johannes Kepler.

1600—Giordano Bruno is burned at the stake for heresy.

1616—*On the Revolutions of the Heavenly Spheres* is placed on the Index.

1642–1727—Life of Isaac Newton.

1781—Uranus is discovered.

1820—The Catholic Church removes *On the Revolutions of the Heavenly Spheres* from the Index.

1846—Neptune is discovered.

1879–1955—Life of Albert Einstein.

1930—Pluto is discovered.

1959—Arthur Koestler's *The Sleepwalkers* is published.

1969—Man walks on the surface of the moon on July 20.

1992—Kuiper Belt is discovered.

2004—Mars probes uncover conclusive evidence that liquid water existed on the planet's surface at some point in time; Owen Gingerich's *The Book Nobody Read: Chasing the Revolutions of Nicolaus Copernicus* is published.

2005—Eris is discovered.

2006—Pluto is reclassified by the IAU (International Astronomical Union) as a dwarf planet, along with Eris and Ceres.

CHAPTER NOTES

Chapter 1. Awakening Ideas

1. Jan Adamczewski, *Nicolaus Copernicus and His Epoch* (Washington D.C.: Copernicus Society of America, 1973), p. 133.

Chapter 2. A Scholarly Youth

1. Jan Adamczewski, *Nicolaus Copernicus and His Epoch* (Washington D.C.: Copernicus Society of America, 1973), p. 28.

2. Marian Biskup and Jerzy Dobrzycki, *Copernicus: Scholar and Citizen* (Warsaw, Poland: Interpress Publishers, 1972), p. 28.

3. Hermann Kesten, *Copernicus and His World*, trans. by E. B. Ashton and Norbert Gutterman (New York: Roy Publishers, 1945), p. 17.

4. Stephen P. Mizwa, *Nicholas Copernicus 1543–1943* (Port Washington, N.Y.: Kennikat Press, Inc., 1943), p. 36.

5. Jan Adamczewski, *The Towns of Copernicus* (Warsaw, Poland: Interpress Publishers, 1972), p. 26.

6. Ibid., p. 27.

7. Jan Adamczewski, *Nicolaus Copernicus and His Epoch*, p. 109.

8. Jerzy Szperkowicz, *Nicolaus Copernicus 1473–1973*, trans. by Eugene Lepa (Warsaw, Poland: PWN-Polish Scientific Publishers, 1972), p. 37.

9. Kesten, p. 128.

10. Henryk Bietkowski and Wlodzimierz Zonn, *The World of Copernicus*, trans. by Doreen Heaton-Potworowska (Warsaw, Poland: Arkady, 1973), p. 113.

11. Adamczewski, *Nicolaus Copernicus and His Epoch*, p. 57.

12. Maria Bogucka, *Nicholas Copernicus: The Country and Times*, trans. by Leon Szwajcer (Wroclaw, Poland: The Ossolinski State Publishing House, 1973), p. 116.

13. Kesten, p. 92.

14. Bogucka, p. 122.

15. Wanda M. Stachiewicz, *Copernicus and His World* (New York: Polish Institute of Arts and Sciences in America, Inc., 1972), p. 30.

16. Kesten, p. 106.

17. Angus Armitage, *Copernicus: The Founder of Modern Astronomy* (New York: Dorset Press, 1990), p. 50.

18. Szperkowicz, pp. 32–34.

19. Biskup and Dobrzycki, p. 43.

20. Bietkowski and Zonn, p. 72.

21. Armitage, p. 50.

22. Kesten, p. 245.

23. Bietkowski and Zonn, p. 88.

24. Adamczewski, *Nicolaus Copernicus and His Epoch*, p. 97.

25. Bogucka, p. 171.

26. Biskup and Dobrzycki, pp. 48–49.

27. Nicolaus Copernicus, *On the Revolutions of the Heavenly Spheres*, trans. by C. G. Wallis, *Great Books of the Western World*, vol. 16 (Chicago: Encyclopedia Britannica, 1952), p. 509.

28. Ibid., pp. 793–794.

Chapter 3. A Radical Theory

1. John North, *The Norton History of Astronomy and Cosmology* (New York: W. W. Norton & Company, 1995), pp. 67–70.

2. Ibid., p. 81.

3. Ibid., pp. 106–120.

4. Nicolaus Copernicus, *On the Revolutions of the Heavenly Spheres*, trans. by C. G. Wallis, *Great Books of the Western World*, vol. 16 (Chicago: Encyclopedia Britannica, 1952), p. 507.

5. North, pp. 85–86.

6. Hermann Kesten, *Copernicus and His World*, trans. by E. B. Ashton and Norbert Gutterman (New York: Roy Publishers, 1945), pp. 175–176.

7. Copernicus, p. 518.

8. Ibid., p. 516.

9. Ibid., p. 521.

10. Ibid., p. 526.

11. Kesten, *Copernicus and His World*, p. 275.

12. Ibid., pp. 196–197.

Chapter 4. The Multitalented Canon

1. Angus Armitage, *Copernicus: The Founder of Modern Astronomy* (New York: Dorset Press, 1990), p. 52.

2. Jan Adamczewski, *The Towns of Copernicus* (Warsaw, Poland: Interpress Publishers, 1972), p. 106.

3. Marian Biskup and Jerzy Dobrzycki, *Copernicus: Scholar and Citizen* (Warsaw, Poland: Interpress Publishers, 1972), p. 62.

4. Hermann Kesten, *Copernicus and His World*, trans. by E. B. Ashton and Norbert Gutterman (New York: Roy Publishers, 1945), p. 72.

5. Adamczewski, *The Towns of Copernicus*, p. 163.

6. Jerzy Szperkowicz, *Nicolaus Copernicus 1473–1973*, trans. by Eugene Lepa (Warsaw, Poland: PWN-Polish Scientific Publishers, 1972), p. 46.

7. Biskup, p. 66.

8. Ibid., p. 65.

9. Ibid., p. 65.

10. Ibid., p. 99.

11. Adamczewski, *The Towns of Copernicus*, p. 128.

12. Angus Armitage, *The World of Copernicus* (New York: Mentor/New American Library, 1947), p. 75.

13. Biskup, p. 49.

14. Max Caspar, *Kepler*. trans. by C. Doris Hellman (New York: Abelard-Schuman, 1959), p. 229.

15. Armitage, *The World of Copernicus*, p. 85.

16. Biskup, p. 100.

17. Gloria Skurzynski, *On Time: From Seasons to Split Seconds* (Washington, D.C.: National Geographic Society, 2000), p. 18.

18. Maria Bogucka, *Nicholas Copernicus: The Country and Times*, trans. by Leon Szwajcer (Wroclaw, Poland: The Ossolinski State Publishing House, 1973), p. 6.

19. Jan Adamczewski, *Nicolaus Copernicus and His Epoch* (Washington, D.C.: Copernicus Society of America, 1973), p. 126.

20. Biskup, pp. 86–90.

21. Adamczewski, *Nicolaus Copernicus and His Epoch*, p. 124.

22. Adamczewski, *The Towns of Copernicus*, p. 126.

23. Armitage, *The World of Copernicus*, p. 98.

24. Adamczewski, *The Towns of Copernicus*, p. 146.

25. Wanda M. Stachiewicz, *Copernicus and His World* (New York: Polish Institute of Arts and Sciences in America, Inc., 1972), p. 34.

26. Bogucka, p. 147.

27. Henryk Bietkowski and Wlodzimierz Zonn, *The World of Copernicus*, trans. by Doreen Heaton-Potworowska (Warsaw, Poland: Arkady, 1973), p. 125.

28. Biskup, p. 70.

29. Bogucka, p. 159.

30. Adamczewski, *Nicolaus Copernicus and His Epoch*, p. 116.

31. Armitage, *Copernicus and His World*, p. 62.

32. Adamczewski, *Nicolaus Copernicus and His Epoch*, p. 115.

33. Ibid.

Chapter 5. Labor of a Lifetime

1. Robert A. Hatch, "Heliocentric Models of the World," n.d., <http://www.clas.ufl.edu/users/rhatch/08-0COP5-dgr-e-s.html> (February 8, 2001).

2. Jan Adamczewski, *Nicolaus Copernicus and His Epoch* (Washington D.C.: Copernicus Society of America, 1973), p. 144.

3. Jerzy Szperkowicz, *Nicolaus Copernicus 1473–1973*, trans. by Eugene Lepa (Warsaw, Poland: PWN-Polish Scientific Publishers, 1972), p. 73.

4. Adamczewski, *Nicolaus Copernicus and His Epoch*, p. 148.

5. Hermann Kesten, *Copernicus and His World*, trans. by E. B. Ashton and Norbert Gutterman (New York: Roy Publishers, 1945), p. vii.

6. Adamczewski, *Nicolaus Copernicus and His Epoch*, p. 148.

7. Angus Armitage, *The World of Copernicus* (New York: Mentor/New American Library, 1947), p. 99.

8. Henryk Bietkowski and Wlodzimierz Zonn, *The World of Copernicus*, trans. by Doreen Heaton-Potworowska (Warsaw, Poland: Arkady, 1973), p. 145.

9. Nicolaus Copernicus, *On the Revolutions of the Heavenly Spheres*, trans. by C. G. Wallis. *Great Books of the Western World*, vol. 16 (Chicago: Encyclopedia Britannica, 1952), p. 506.

10. Adamczewski, *Nicolaus Copernicus and His Epoch*, pp. 151–152.

11. Copernicus, p. 507.

12. Kesten, *Copernicus and His World*, p. 277.

13. Ibid., p. 16.

14. Armitage, *The World of Copernicus*, p. 105.

15. Marian Biskup and Jerzy Dobrzycki, *Copernicus: Scholar and Citizen* (Warsaw, Poland: Interpress Publishers, 1972), p. 106.

16. Kesten, *Copernicus and His World*, p. 302.

17. Ibid., p. 294.

18. Biskup, p. 117.

19. Armitage, *The World of Copernicus*, p. 102.

20. Biskup, p. 116.

21. Adamczewski, *Nicolaus Copernicus and His Epoch.*, p. 156.

22. Biskup, pp. 17–18.

23. Kesten, *Copernicus and His World*, p. 303.

24. Jan Adamczewski, *The Towns of Copernicus* (Warsaw, Poland: Interpress Publishers, 1972), p. 164.

Chapter 6. The Legacy of Copernicus

1. Hermann Kesten, *Copernicus and His World*, trans. by E. B. Ashton and Norbert Gutterman (New York: Roy Publishers, 1945), p. 320.

2. Jan Adamczewski, *Nicolaus Copernicus and His Epoch* (Washington D.C.: Copernicus Society of America, 1973), pp. 144–145.

3. Kesten, *Copernicus and His World*, p. 318.

4. Ibid., pp. 304–305.

5. Ibid., pp. 330–331.

6. Ibid., pp. 323–325.

7. Ibid., p. 321.

8. Ibid., p. 333.

9. Ibid., p. 340.

10. Ibid., p. 354.

11. Ibid., p. 369.

12. Ibid., p. 349.

13. Jan Adamczewski, *Nicolaus Copernicus and His Epoch* (Washington, D.C.: Copernicus Society of America, 1973), p. 158.

14. Ibid.

15. Kesten, *Copernicus and His World*, p. 376.

16. Owen Gingerich, *The Book Nobody Read: Chasing the Revolutions of Nicolaus Copernicus* (New York: Walker & Company, 2004), p. 145.

17. Angus Armitage, *The World of Copernicus* (New York: Mentor/New American Library, 1947), pp. 147–149.

18. Adamczewski, *Nicolaus Copernicus and His Epoch*, 159.

19. Kesten, *Copernicus and His World*, p. 316.

20. Gingerich, p. 216.

21. Stephen P. Mizwa, *Nicholas Copernicus 1543–1943* (Port Washington, N.Y.: Kennikat Press, Inc., 1943), p. 24.

22. Adamczewski, *Nicolaus Copernicus and His Epoch*, p. 159.

23. Kesten, *Copernicus and His World*, p. viii.

Chapter 7. Continued Revolutions

1. Copernicus, *On the Revolutions of the Heavenly Spheres*, trans. By J. J. O'Connor and E. F. Robertson, School of Mathematics and Statistics, University of Saint Andrews, Scotland, November 2002, <http://www-history.mcs.st-andrews.ac.uk/Biographies/Copernicus.html> (July, 2007).

2. Arthur Koestler, *The Sleep Walkers: A History of Man's Changing Vision of the Universe* (New York: Macmillan, 1959), p. 191.

3. Owen Gingerich, *The Book Nobody Read: Chasing the Revolutions of Nicolaus Copernicus* (New York: Walker & Company, 2004), p. 129.

4. Ibid., p. 121.

5. Ibid., p. 145.

6. Peter DeMarco, "Book Quest Took Him Around the Globe," *The Boston Globe*, April 13, 2004, <http://www.boston.com/news/education/higher/articles/2004/04/13/book_quest_took_him_around_the_globe/> (April 6, 2008).

7. "Pluto," The Nine Planets Solar System Tour, n.d., <http://www.nineplanets.org/pluto.html> (April 7, 2008).

8. "The IAU draft definition of 'planet' and 'plutons,'" *IAU Website*, August 16, 2006, <http://www.iau.org/iau0601.424.0.html> (April 7, 2008).

9. S. Alan Stern, "OpEd: And Copernicus Smiled," *Space News*, August 29, 2005, http://www.space.com/spacenews/archive05/SternOpEd_082905.html> (April 2, 2008).

Activity 4

1. From "Building and Using an Astrolabe" by James Zuhn, courtesy of the Texas Historical Commission; the original activity is on the Internet at http://www.thc.state.tx.us/journeys/Astrolabe.html.

GLOSSARY

almanac—Any book containing tables on the times and locations of the rising and setting of the sun, the stars, and the planets.

astrolabe—An instrument used to find latitude (distance north or south of the equator) by locating the North Star and measuring angles.

astrology—The study of the supposed effect the positions of stars and planets have on people's lives.

astronomy—The science that studies the motions of the moon, the stars, the planets, and the sun.

axis—A straight line about which a figure rotates.

conjunction—When two celestial bodies appear to line up vertically in the sky.

dwarf planet—A celestial body (one that is neither a star nor a satellite) that orbits a star and possesses enough mass to produce sufficient gravity to give it a round shape, but has not cleared its surroundings of other planetesimals.

ellipse—A closed plane curve resembling a stretched-out circle.

epicycle—A circle whose center is a point on a larger circle.

equant—A balancing point between two other points or objects.

General Theory of Relativity—Theory stating that gravity curves the fabric of space-time.

geocentric—The theory that the earth is the center of the universe or solar system.

geometry—The field of mathematics that studies lines, angles, and two- and three-dimensional figures (such as squares and cubes).

heliocentric—The theory that the sun is at the center of the universe or solar system.

heresy—A religious belief that goes so much against standard teachings, it is considered dangerous.

horoscope—A prediction of the future made by an astrologer, based on the positions of stars and planets, usually at the time of a person's birth.

hypothesis—A theory; a suggested explanation for a phenomenon, which needs to be proved.

latitude—The number of degrees north or south of the equator a place is.

leprosy—A skin disease.

manuscript—A handwritten book.

Middle Ages—The period of history between the ancient and modern periods, about 500 to 1500 A.D.

model—A detailed explanation of a phenomenon.

occultation—When one celestial body passes in front of another.

parallax—The angle formed when the same object is viewed from two different points.

philosophy—The study of logic and reality.

planet—A celestial body (one that is neither a star nor a satellite) that orbits a star, possesses enough mass to produce sufficient gravity to give it a round shape, and has cleared its surroundings of other planetesimals.

planetesimals—Solid objects in the rotating disks of the dense gas, dust, and debris surrounding a star.

Renaissance—A movement beginning in the four-teenth century in Europe that emphasized curiosity, learning, the arts, and the recovery of ancient texts.

retrograde motion—The apparent backward move-ment of a planet, such as Mars, when it is overtaken in its orbit by another planet, such as Earth.

spheres—Three-dimensional forms based on circles. Ancient philosophers and astronomers believed that the universe was made up of a series of spheres, one inside the other.

telescope—An observational instrument made from a series of precisely placed lenses that makes distant objects appear closer.

theory—A proposed explanation for a set of phenomena.

triquetrum—An instrument made of three hinged piec-es of wood; it was used to measure angles in observations of distant objects.

FURTHER READING

Farndon, John. *From Ptolemy's Spheres to Dark Energy: Discovering the Universe*. Chicago, Ill.: Heinemann Library, 2007.

Gingerich, Owen, and James MacLachlan. *Nicolaus Copernicus: Making the Earth a Planet*. New York: Oxford University Press, 2005.

Gingram, Scott. *Giants of Science: Nicolaus Copernicus*. Farmington Hills, Mich.: Blackbirch Press, 2004.

Miller, Ron. *Recentering the Universe: The Radical Theories of Copernicus, Kepler, Galileo, and Newton*. New York: Lerner Publishing Group, 2013.

Repcheck, Jack. *Copernicus' Secret: How the Scientific Revolution Began*. New York: Simon and Schuster, 2007.

Sakolsky, Josh. *Copernicus and Modern Astronomy*. New York: Rosen Publishing Group, 2004.

Somervill, Barbara A. *Nicolaus Copernicus: Father of Modern Astronomy*. Mankato, Minn.: Compass Point Books, 2005.

INDEX